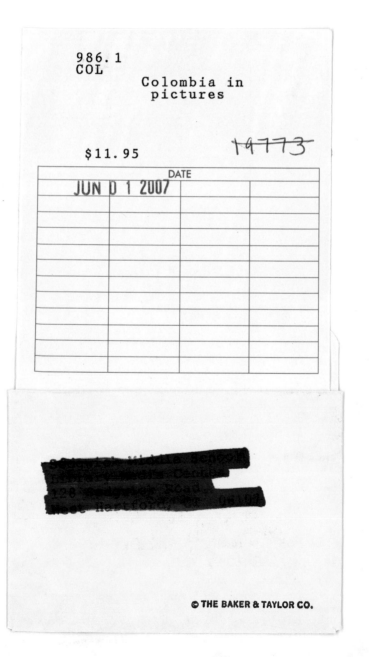

COLOMBIA

...in Pictures

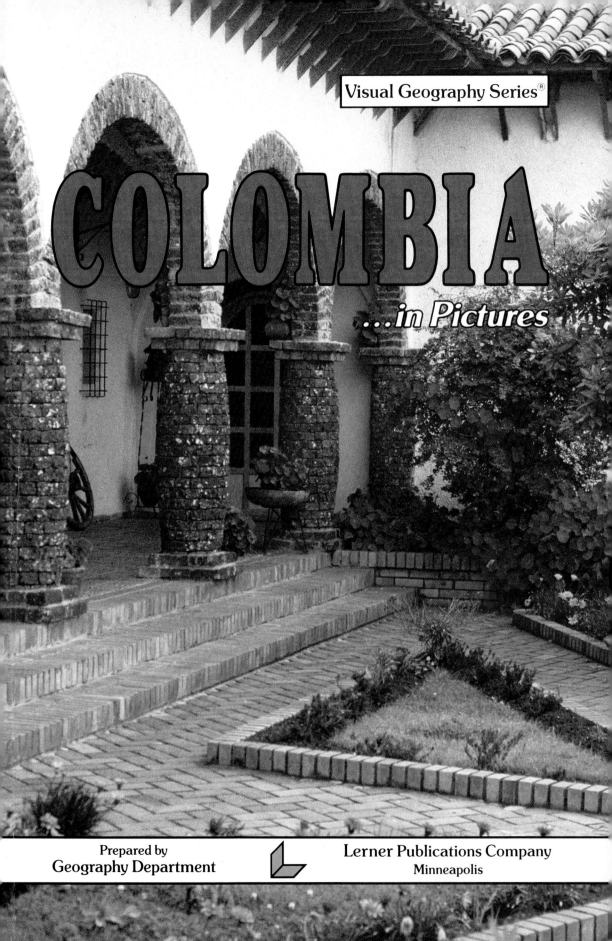

Visual Geography Series®

COLOMBIA
...in Pictures

Prepared by
Geography Department

Lerner Publications Company
Minneapolis

Courtesy of World Bank

Two young Colombians enjoy a swim near Montería.

This book is an all-new edition in the Visual Geography Series. Previous editions were published by Sterling Publishing Company, New York City. The text, set in 10/12 Century Textbook, is fully revised and updated, and new photographs, maps, charts, and captions have been added.

LIBRARY OF CONGRESS CATALOGING-IN-PUBLICATION DATA

Colombia in pictures.

(Visual geography series)
Rev. ed. of: Colombia in pictures / prepared by Martha Murray Sumwalt.
Includes index.
Summary: An introduction to the geography, history, people, government, and economy of the fourth largest country in South America.
1. Colombia. [1. Colombia] I. Sumwalt, Martha Murray. Colombia in pictures. II. Lerner Publications Company. Geography Dept. III. Series: Visual geography series (Minneapolis, Minn.)
F2258.C66 1987 986.1 86-33816
ISBN 0-8225-1816-4 (lib. bdg.)

International Standard Book Number: 0-8225-1810-4
Library of Congress Catalog Card Number: 86-33816

VISUAL GEOGRAPHY SERIES®

Publisher
Harry Jonas Lerner
Associate Publisher
Nancy M. Campbell
Executive Series Editor
Mary M. Rodgers
Assistant Series Editor
Gretchen Bratvold
Editorial Assistant
Nora W. Kniskern
Illustrations Editors
Nathan A. Haverstock
Karen A. Sirvaitis
Consultants/Contributors
Dr. Ruth F. Hale
Nathan A. Haverstock
Sandra K. Davis
Designer
Jim Simondet
Cartographer
Carol F. Barrett
Indexer
Kristine S. Schubert
Production Manager
Gary J. Hansen

Independent Picture Service

A craftsperson weaves fibers into a strong matting.

Acknowledgments

Title page photo by Amandus Schneider.

Elevation contours adapted from *The Times Atlas of the World,* seventh comprehensive edition (New York: Times Books, 1985).

3 4 5 6 7 8 9 10 96 95 94 93 92 91 90

The Spanish architectural designs imposed on towns throughout the Spanish colonies are evident at Barichara, an Andean village established in 1742 about 200 miles north of Bogotá. Each block of the village is a hollow square of dwellings with red-tiled roofs that have been built around a central patio shared by all families living in the block.

Introduction

During the last 30 years, Colombia has provided the world with a rare example of the power of compromise. As one of the sponsors of the Contador peace treaty, Colombia ranks as a leader of regional nations trying to ease tensions in Central America. Tensions within its own borders, however, have grown, as the government has strengthened its war against the country's powerful drug cartels.

Like its neighbors in Latin America, Colombia emerged from three centuries of Spanish rule as a divided nation, with a minority of rich people and many poor people. Colombia's effort to develop industries and jobs was complicated by its mountain-

ous geography. Building roads and schools on this rugged terrain proved difficult and costly. Following independence in 1810, Colombians were divided about where and how scarce governmental funds should be invested. Bitter differences arose between Conservative and Liberal political parties about the form the national government should take and about whether it should be loosely or centrally organized.

In 1948 these root issues—fanned by the assassination of a Liberal leader and growing discontent with a succession of corrupt governments—sparked violence in the capital city of Bogotá. *La Violencia* (the violence), as the turmoil came to be called, spread to the countryside and did not end until the late 1950s. Two hundred thousand people—mostly rural workers—lost their lives. In 1957 Colombians decided by popular vote to stop the political feuding that had brought about such destruction. They formed the National Front, which allowed Conservatives and Liberals to share power equally for the next 16 years. The presidency alternated between the two groups, and each administration consisted of members from both parties. The National Front arrangement lasted until 1986.

With a workable political system in place, Colombia has been able to draw on its strengths. These include abundant natural resources and a vigorous people with strong religious, political, and family ties. Colombia has nearly a dozen large, developing cities. Their progress has been achieved regionally—not through a design from faraway Bogotá.

The past three decades have seen dramatic advances in Colombia's production of fuel, in its manufacturing capacity, and in its commodity exports. At the same time, the country's farmers have expanded their production to include nontraditional crops to make the country largely self-sufficient in food. On the negative side, Colombia produces and markets illegal drugs, mainly to buyers in the United States. Though successive Colombian governments have tried, they have been unable to stop this illegal activity. Drug trafficking reportedly produces as much income for Colombia as all other parts of the economy combined.

A 1984 truce between the administration of former president Belisario Betancur Cuartas and four of the country's seven guerrilla groups manifests Colombia's commitment to compromise. Under this agreement rebels in arms received a general pardon and a chance to participate in the political process in return for laying down their weapons. Yet since the truce was agreed upon, 2,500 people have been killed.

Colombia's president Virgilio Barco Vargas declared upon election in 1986 that he aimed to address the nation's domestic woes. These problems included high unemployment, widespread poverty, unequal distribution of wealth, and the still-strong guerrilla movement that wished to force reforms violently. But by 1989, Barco's attention turned to the international problem of Colombia's powerful minority of drug lords. In that year, they killed Senator Luis Carlos Galán, a popular contender in the 1990 presidential election. They also assassinated dozens of judges and officials responsible for enforcing Colombia's drug laws. Complicating the efforts of the Colombian government is a lack of money to fight the cartels. This problem worsened in July 1989 when an international coffee pact was suspended, drastically reducing income earned from the country's main legal export. As a result, President Barco has focused on international issues that gravely affect Colombians.

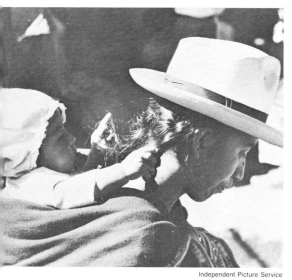

An Indian woman carries her child on her back in a securely tied shawl.

Gently rolling hills devoted largely to agriculture are among Colombia's many topographical features.

1) The Land

The Republic of Colombia, fourth largest country in South America, is the only South American nation that has the advantage of coastlines on both the Atlantic and Pacific oceans. To the northwest, Colombia borders Panama (once a Colombian province); Venezuela shares Colombia's northeastern border. To the southeast is Brazil, and to the south are Ecuador and Peru.

With an area of 439,737 square miles, Colombia is about equal in size to the states of Texas, Oklahoma, and New Mexico combined. Colombia's terrain is extremely varied, including high mountains, rolling hills, broad plateaus, and vast, low plains. Until recent times the ruggedness of much of Colombia's land was an obstacle to the development of the country's wealth of natural resources.

Mountains

The Andes dominate the western third of Colombia. Most Colombians live in the valleys and plateaus of the west that are divided by three parallel mountain chains, which extend north to south through the country. The first range is the Cordillera Occidental, or western range of the Colombian Andes, which is separated from the Cordillera Central—the second and highest

9

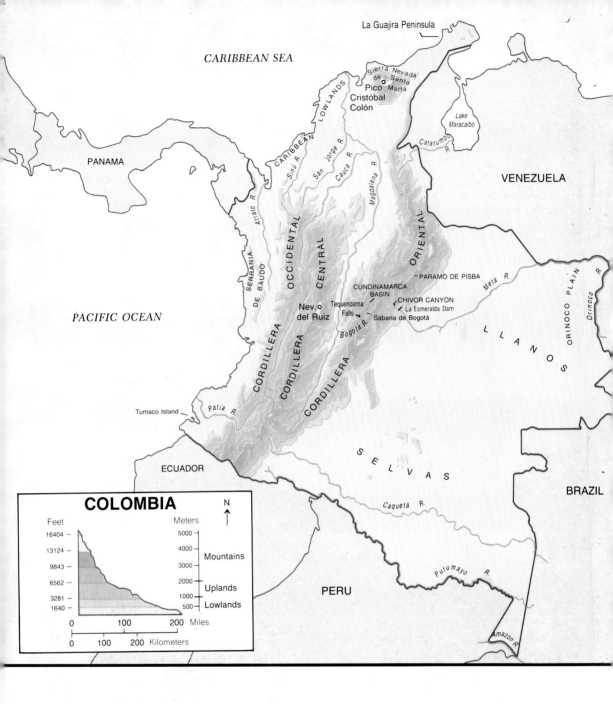

CARIBBEAN SEA

La Guajira Peninsula

Sierra Nevada de Santa Marta

Pico Cristóbal Colón

PANAMA

Lake Maracaibo

Catatumbo R.

VENEZUELA

CARIBBEAN LOWLANDS

Sinú R.
San Jorge R.
Cauca R.
Magdalena R.

Atrato R.

SERRANIA DE BAUDO

CORDILLERA OCCIDENTAL

CORDILLERA CENTRAL

CORDILLERA ORIENTAL

PARAMO DE PISBA

CUNDINAMARCA BASIN

CHIVOR CANYON

La Esmeralda Dam

Meta R.

ORINOCO PLAIN

Orinoco R.

PACIFIC OCEAN

Nev. del Ruiz

Tequendama Falls

Sabana de Bogotá

Bogotá R.

L L A N O S

Tumaco Island

Patía R.

CORDILLERA

S E L V A S

ECUADOR

BRAZIL

Caquetá R.

COLOMBIA

N

Feet		Meters	
16404 —		5000 —	
13124 —		4000 —	Mountains
9843 —		3000 —	
6562 —		2000 —	Uplands
3281 —		1000 —	
1640 —		500 —	Lowlands

| 0 | 100 | 200 | Miles |
| 0 | 100 | 200 | Kilometers |

PERU

Putumayo R.

Amazon R.

Andean range—by a valley. The third mountain range is the Cordillera Oriental, which extends northward from the Caquetá River all the way to the lowlands of Lake Maracaibo. En route to the lake, this range forms a spectacular backdrop for the capital city of Bogotá.

The mountains of the Cordillera Occidental rise to heights of 6,000 to 10,000 feet but are dwarfed by summits of the Cordillera Central, whose snowcapped volcanoes extend upward to more than 18,000 feet. The lowest of the three major ranges, the Cordillera Oriental, averages about 7,000 feet above sea level. The highest peaks in Colombia—including Pico Cristóbal Colón at 19,020 feet—are found in an isolated mountain chain near the Caribbean called the Sierra Nevada de Santa Marta. A smaller range—the Serranía de Baudó—exists off the Pacific coast.

In 1985 the Nevado del Ruiz, a long-dormant volcano in the Cordillera Central, suddenly erupted and within hours left more than 45,000 people dead or injured. Avalanches of gray ash and mud virtually destroyed the town of Armero, which once had a population of about 25,000. This eruption rates as one of the worst volcanic disasters in recorded history— roughly equivalent to the explosion of Mount Vesuvius, which destroyed Pompeii, Italy, in A.D. 79. Since the eruption, many of the survivors have moved to nearby Guayabal, where international relief organizations have built new houses and schools to accommodate the refugees.

Plateaus and Grasslands

The Cordillera Central broadens in the vicinity of Bogotá to become a great plateau known as the Cundinamarca Basin. The densely populated region of Antioquia lies to the northwest, between the Cordillera Central and the Cordillera Occidental and along a tributary of the Cauca River. This area is famous for its industrialization, coffee production, and important mineral deposits. Near the junction of the Cauca and Magdalena rivers, the Cordillera Central gives way to the Caribbean coastal lowlands.

North and east of the three mountain chains are the llanos, or grassy lowlands, of the Orinoco Plain and the Caribbean coast. The selvas, or rain-forests, lie to the southeast and in the Amazon Basin. Colombia's ciénagas—shallow lakes that occupy much of the coastal area east of the Magdalena River—evaporate sufficiently during the dry season (November through June) to be used for grazing. While these lowlands make up over half of the country, they contain less than 5 percent of the population.

Despite its high elevation, the large plateau around Bogotá—called the Cundinamarca Basin—contains grasslands and shallow lakes.

Rivers

The course of Colombia's rivers is largely determined by the north-south pattern of its mountain ranges. The Patía River, in southwestern Colombia, is the only one that has forced its way through the cordilleras to flow to the Pacific. The Magdalena—South America's fourth longest river—twists between two branches of the Cordillera Occidental until it reaches the Caribbean Sea. With almost 900 miles of navigable waterway, the Magdalena is Colombia's chief commercial river. Other rivers are the Atrato, running to the Pacific between two smaller sections of the Cordillera Occidental; the Cauca, a tributary of the Magdalena draining a fertile valley between the western and central ranges; the Meta, which originates south of Bogotá and proceeds eastward to the Orinoco River; and the Caquetá, in the southeast, which flows eastward to the Amazon.

The Cauca River runs through one of the richest agricultural sections of western Colombia and supports a large hydroelectric power complex run by the Cauca Valley Authority.

Small waterways—usually tributaries of Colombia's many large rivers—flow through much of the nation.

This section of the 900-mile-long Magdalena River is near San Agustín in south central Colombia.

Photo by Don Irish

Although the Orinoco and Amazon rivers do not lie within Colombia's boundaries, the country borders on the Orinoco and on the Putumayo—a tributary of the Amazon. Moreover, Colombia has a very short stretch of the Amazon itself near the river port of Leticia, where Brazil, Colombia, and Peru meet. The huge Amazon-Orinoco Basin, which contains more square miles than the United States, is one of the world's few remaining sizable tropical rain-forests.

The Amazon is fed by eight major tributaries and numerous smaller ones, many of which flow through Colombia's selvas and llanos. The Amazon Basin, which lies partly in southeastern Colombia, is like a huge inland sea dotted with islands, many of which are underwater during the rainy season. In times of flooding, the Amazon overflows onto a 50-mile-wide plain, carrying huge chunks of earth and vegetation toward the Pacific Ocean. This massive river is navigable by oceangoing ships as far inland as Leticia in Colombia and Iquitos in Peru—over 2,300 miles west of its mouth on the Atlantic Ocean.

Climate

Like most mountainous countries near the equator, Colombia's climate changes with altitude. The tierra caliente, or hot zone, is measured from sea level to 3,500 feet and has average daily temperatures of about 80° F. Here annual rainfall varies according to the height of the mountain slopes, but the humidity is usually high. Arid La Guajira Peninsula receives only about 25 inches of rain annually, mostly in a four-month rainy season from June through September. The dry season in the

Caribbean lowlands usually lasts from October to March. The tierra templada, or temperate zone, from 3,500 to 6,500 feet above sea level, has annual temperatures of 65° to 70° F, with a yearly rainfall of 40 to 100 inches. The tierra fría, or cold zone, from 6,500 feet upward, extends from the highest mountain forests to the windy, treeless paramos (alpine plains) near the mountaintops, which can be used only for grazing. The snow line begins at about 15,000 feet.

Flora and Fauna

As more roads are built and new areas are opened for development, the need for conservation of South America's phenomenal plant and animal life becomes vital. Colombia's government is making an effort to preserve and protect the nation's wildlife and vegetation, but effective conservation is costly. With the rate of destruction now measured in acres, South America's wilderness is rapidly becoming endangered.

Despite the losses, South America still contains a unique mixture of old and new forms of life, perhaps more distinctive than those of any other continent except Australia. Colombia's flora and fauna reflect its position at the junction of Central and South America, where two continental landmasses meet. The isolation of Colombia's valleys, which are caught between steep mountain ranges, cause contrasts of altitude and climate and further contribute to the nation's many varieties of plants and animals.

VEGETATION

Vegetation in Colombia is diverse, ranging from lush tropical growth to stunted alpine shrubs. Its forests yield dyewoods, vanilla, tanning agents, and medical products, such as quinine and balsam. Hardwoods like oak, cedar, walnut, mahogany, and brazilwood also thrive in Colombian forests. Colombia's tropical rainforests are thick with ferns, bamboo, orchids, rubber trees, coconut palms, and tropical fruits.

Courtesy of Klaus Paysan

A colorful macaw clings to its perch in a Colombian forest. Macaws have very strong beaks and harsh voices, and adults mate for life.

14

Warm, saltwater lagoons along the coast support swamp grass, reedy marshes, and mangroves with scattered trees along the river banks. Toward the interior, the vegetation changes. In the Magdalena River Valley, there are areas of thorny brush, tufted grass, and low trees, which shed only some of their leaves at a time. Areas of the Cauca River Valley in the southwest have woodlands up to elevations of 6,000 feet above sea level.

Most of Colombia's lower mountain slopes are covered with forests of pine, oak, and other evergreen or leaf-shedding trees. In the coffee plantations of this temperate zone, various small trees are planted to shade the coffee bushes. The eucalyptus, which was imported from Australia, also grows well at this level. High on the cold, windy paramos of the tierra fría are woodlands with a dwarfed vegetation of vines, shrubs, mosses, tufted grass, and resinous woody plants. Higher

still are the bare summits and ever-present snow of the tallest mountains.

WILDLIFE

The fauna of Colombia includes many curiosities. For example, the Amazon and Orinoco rivers and their tributaries contain freshwater species—including dolphins and stingrays—usually found only in the open sea. There are tiny fish, like the guppy and the neon tetra, and giant ones, like the arapaima, which is among the largest freshwater fish in the world. Besides tarpon, sharks, sawfish, and electric eels, Colombia's waters are home to dangerous piranhas, which travel in schools of 100 to 1,000 and can tear the flesh off an animal as neatly as a razor.

Among Colombia's many reptiles are the dreaded anaconda—a constrictor water snake—numerous lizards, crocodiles, and caimans. Most of the big game has fled into the forests and mountains. The gray-

In 1936 the first neon tetras were exported from their habitats in the Amazon areas of South America. The bright blue line that runs the length of their bodies varies in color depending on the light.

Courtesy of Klaus Paysan

15

Tapirs live in dense forests and swamps and feed on fruit and foliage. Overzealous hunters have reduced the tapir population in South America nearly to extinction.

brown puma stalks the hills and plains, while the spotted ocelot and jaguar prefer living near streams where they can feed on water animals. One of the most unique looking creatures is the stout tapir, with its slender legs, dainty hoofs, and long flexible snout. More varieties of bat—among them the vampire bat—are found in Colombia than in any other place in the world.

The country also has about 1,500 species of birds. They vary in size from the tiny hummingbird, which flies backwards and sideways, to the large harpy eagle, which feeds on sloths, monkeys, opossums, and guinea pigs. The shiny green jacamar is one of Colombia's most beautiful tropical birds; another is the bright cotinga, which flits through the jungle like a blazing comet. Other brightly hued birds are the macaw, tanager, parakeet, and the exotic toucan, with its enormous, turned-down beak shaped like a lobster's claw.

Major Cities

Colombia has more than a dozen sizable cities with populations in excess of 200,000 people. These secondary cities check the power of the capital city of Bogotá.

Located in a high valley called the Sabana de Bogotá, at an elevation of more than 8,500 feet, Bogotá has a moist, spring-like climate, with an average year-round temperature of about 58° F. The population, now at about five million, is rapidly increasing, due partly to the arrival of many citizens from the countryside. This influx has created crowded slums, called *tugurios,* of makeshift housing where unemployment, poverty, and crime rates are high. Without adequate food or shelter, children from these areas often run away from home and become beggars and petty thieves on the city streets.

As the political hub of Colombia, Bogotá is also the artistic, cultural, and intellectual capital. Founded by the Spanish in 1538, Bogotá is one of the oldest cities in the Western Hemisphere and contains many stately colonial homes, churches, and universities. Narrow streets lined with balconied buildings spread out from Plaza Bolívar, the heart of old Bogotá. Circling the plaza are the city hall, national capitol, cardinal's palace, and cathedral.

A cable car rises to the top of Monserrate, a peak that provides an excellent view of the city. At the foot of this mountain is Quinta de Bolívar, the former home of Colombia's liberator, now a museum with beautiful gardens. Also near Bogotá are the Zipaquirá salt mines and Tequendama Falls; the latter plunges 450 feet into a dense, green forest. The Zipaquirá

Photo by Amandus Schneider

The site of the Tequendama Falls is about 10 miles from Bogotá. Before the source of the falls – the Bogotá River – was dammed for hydroelectric purposes, the 427-foot-high falls rushed downward all year round.

Photo by Amandus Schneider

Bogotá lies in an 8,563-foot-high plateau within sight of the Cordillera Oriental. Its Spanish colonial architecture now stands alongside many modern buildings.

17

mines are believed to have enough salt to supply the world for a hundred years.

About 150 miles west of Bogotá is the rich coffee and mining district of Antioquia. Its main city, Medellín, is Colombia's second largest urban area and is an industrial hub known especially for its textile mills. Although not as clean as it was before its recent population explosion, Medellín has a pleasant climate and dramatic mountain scenery. The city was settled by Europeans in the late 1600s. The population reached 500,000 within 200 years, though there was little immigration from abroad after 1700. Today almost two million people live in Medellín. Early settlers quickly became self-sufficient farmers, and the region is now the leading coffee-growing area in Colombia.

Medellín also has the unfortunate distinction of being the home of one of the largest cocaine-selling groups. It reputedly handles 80 percent of the world market of this dangerous drug.

Colombia's third largest city is Cali, located in the fertile Cauca River Valley, some 200 miles south of Medellín. Cali dates its economic growth from the period of La Violencia, when thousands of Colombians sought refuge in this city to escape rural warfare.

In 1940 Cali had just 100,000 people, but by the late 1980s its population had grown by more than 1,500 percent to 1.5 million people. The city is surrounded by level lands backed up against the mountains, where sugar, cotton, rice, and coffee are grown and cattle are raised. Because of its large work force and progressive local leadership, metropolitan Cali has attracted many industries. Headquartered in Cali is Carvajal S.A., a leading publisher of Spanish-language books.

Secondary Cities

About 60 miles south of Cali is Popayán, which contains Colombia's most-treasured examples of Spanish colonial art and ar-

Independent Picture Service

The large city of Cali in western Colombia has several splendid churches. La Ermita (the Hermitage) is gothic in style.

chitecture. Popayán is the most important religious site in Colombia. Its vivid, torch-lit Easter celebration, which dates back to the conquistadors, attracts pilgrims from all over Colombia each year.

Cartagena is not far from the large port of Barranquilla on the Caribbean Sea. As a former gathering place for Spanish treasure fleets, Cartagena is one of the most historic and picturesque towns in South America. The area boasts some of the finest examples of sixteenth-century Spanish architecture in the Western Hemisphere. The old city is heavily fortified by 16 miles of protective wall, which is 50 feet wide in some places and encloses narrow streets and pastel-tinted adobe buildings. The fortress of San Felipe de Barajas, a huge structure built on an island and connected to the mainland by bridges and secret underground passages, is said to be the most complex work of military architecture ever erected by Spain in the Americas.

Courtesy of Inter-American Development Bank

Like other fast-growing cities of Colombia, Medellín is unable to keep up with the demand for new housing. Moreover, it faces mountain barriers in nearly all directions. This has seriously hampered the city's attempts to expand. Its high level of industrialization has caused some smog to develop. Consequently, the city is dirtier than it once was.

Independent Picture Service

Sailing boats gather in the Caribbean waters off Cartagena. Three centuries ago, these waters were full of treasure-laden cargo ships and well-armed Spanish galleons ready to embark on the long, dangerous trip back to Spain. The last attempt to invade the fortified city was by Britain's Admiral Edward Vernon, who failed to take the fort in 1741 after a 56-day siege.

The Valley of Statues at San Agustín contains hundreds of huge stone figures depicting humans, animals, and gods. Dating from the sixth century B.C., the statues have not yet been associated with any known culture and continue to puzzle archaeologists.

Photo by Don Irish

2) History and Government

According to archaeologists, many Indian groups occupied the territory of what is now Colombia, beginning as long ago as 5,000 B.C. The famous stone ruins of San Agustín in southwestern Colombia date from about 500 B.C. Although these ruins are relatively recent, the culture of the people who carved huge stone figures there still puzzles historians.

Elsewhere in Colombia archaeologists are continuing to make new discoveries.

The 1976 excavation of a 1,500-acre city built about A.D. 900 near Santa Marta provided evidence that many Colombian groups had developed permanent settlements long ago. Advances in farming techniques were also brought to light.

The Chibcha

About a third of Colombia's prehistoric Indians were of the Chibcha tribe and lived mainly in the high Cundinamarca Basin, where Bogotá is located today. Legend relates that Bogotá was named for Bacatá, a Chibchan town or chief. The Chibcha lived in villages and were organized along class lines. Deeply religious, the Chibcha were ruled through a system where rank and status were inherited from the mother.

The Chibcha were subdivided into tribes that occupied their own distinct provinces. Tribes sometimes warred with one another, using darts, shields, blowguns, and wooden clubs as weapons. They were skilled in mining and farming and in the production of handicrafts fashioned from gold and other precious materials—some of which have survived to the present day. They had an effective system for communal ownership of land, under which they grew maize (corn), beans, and potatoes. When the Spaniards arrived, the Chibcha were becoming a unified, centralized society, though they were not yet organized

Photo by Dr. Roma Hoff

On the outskirts of Bogotá, a life-sized statue commemorates Colombia's pre-Columbian Indians.

Courtesy of Museum of Modern Art of Latin America

A sculpted human figure carrying a staff was discovered on Tumaco Island off mainland Colombia's southern coast and dates from around 500 B.C.

enough to offer much resistance to the better-armed invaders.

Discovery and Conquest

Although Colombia owes the origin of its name to Christopher Columbus, it is not known whether he ever touched Colombia's shores. Juan de la Cosa, a later explorer, landed on La Guajira Peninsula in 1499. Alonso de Ojeda led an expedition in 1500 that attempted to establish permanent settlements to serve as bases for future expeditions.

Another Spaniard, Rodrigo de Bastidas, launched the conquest of Colombia—and of the rest of the South American continent—in 1525. Pedro de Heredia's settlement of Cartagena followed in 1533. From

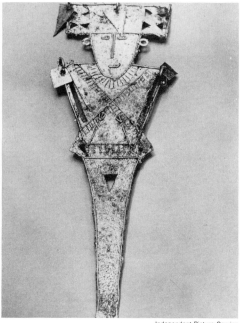

The legend of El Dorado sprang from the wealth of gold objects used by the Indians in South America. This *tunjo,* or religious figure shaped like a human being, was the work of the Chibcha.

Gonzalo Jiménez de Quesada (1495–1579), a Spanish conquistador, led an expedition through Colombia to find El Dorodo—a fabled kingdom.

early villages, the conquistadors later advanced up the Magdalena River toward the Andean plateau.

THE LEGEND OF EL DORADO

Legendary among the Chibchan places of worship were lakes in which tribal leaders took ceremonial purification baths. Reports of these rites and the discovery of gold and emeralds near the coast gave rise to the myth of the fabulous wealth of El Dorado (the golden one). The legend lured the conquistadors to Colombia's interior in search of possible riches. Many Spaniards made fortunes by raiding the huacas—tombs of Indian chieftains—which were filled with precious objects.

Assuming the Chibcha were as wealthy as the Incas and Aztecs, colonial governors organized explorations to the central plateau. Gonzalo Jiménez de Quesada was sent by the governor of Santa Marta on such an expedition. His long trip through dense jungles and steep mountains, which were inhabited by fierce Indians and wild animals, took about nine months. In 1537 the party reached the fertile Cundinamarca Basin, where they founded the town of Santa Fé de Bogotá.

Two other explorers, Nicholas Federmann and Sebastián de Belalcázar, joined Jiménez de Quesada in central Colombia. While traveling down the Magdalena from the Atlantic Ocean, Jiménez de Quesada had seen many blocks of salt, and he began to look for their origin. Federmann, a German adventurer, had just crossed the wide, eastern plains from Venezuela. As a captain for the explorer Francisco Pizarro, Belalcázar was fresh from the conquest of present-day Ecuador. He would have continued up the Pacific coast had he not heard an Indian praising Zipa, the king of gold, who lived in the northeast.

Lured by the legend of El Dorado, early Spanish conquerors forced the Chibcha to mine for gold and emeralds under cruel conditions of enslavement. Despite vague decrees from far-off Spain that encouraged

In a partially cleared forest along Colombia's border with Venezuela, members of the Motilón tribe live together in one huge dwelling, rather than in individual homes.

Throughout the Spanish colonies, the local ethnic groups were put to work digging for precious metals and labored under cruel conditions of slavery.

humane treatment of conquered Indians, the colonists worked them to death.

Subduing groups in remote jungle areas was difficult. The Indians in these areas were often hostile. They knew the terrain far better than the colonists did. The Indians could attack intruders by surprise. As a result, the Spaniards failed to control large areas of the eastern plains and jungles during the colonial period. The Motilôn, one of the few remaining isolated tribes of South America, resist contact with outsiders to this day. From secret mountain hideouts along the Colombia-Venezuela border, the Motilôn have attacked missionaries and other strangers with blowguns and poisoned arrows in fairly recent times.

Colonial Period

In 1549 King Charles V of Spain created a royal audiencia (an administrative body headed by a representative of the king), which had judicial and governmental functions. Within the framework of the audiencia, cabildos (city councils) were set up to govern local municipal affairs. During the period of the audiencia, the Roman Catholic Church, as elsewhere in the Spanish colonies, oversaw religious affairs and education. In Colombia the Church developed into a particularly powerful voice of both the Spanish crown and conservative views in general.

The New Kingdom of Granada—as Colombia was then called—was in turn subject to the Viceroyalty of Peru, which was headquartered in Lima. This arrangement proved awkward because of the long distance separating the states. Also, superiors of the Spanish bureaucracy often delayed making decisions on urgent matters. Nevertheless, the arrangement lasted until 1717, when Spain finally made the New Kingdom of Granada into a separate viceroyalty with jurisdiction over the territories of modern Colombia, Panama, Venezuela, and Ecuador.

Courtesy of Museum of Modern Art of Latin America

The belltower of the cathedral of Barichara overlooks the entire town. Like most Roman Catholic outposts of the colonial period, the cathedral stands at the center of the main square—a reminder of the Church's influence and power.

Between 1564 and 1810, New Granada was ruled by 13 viceroys and 26 presidents, all of whom were appointed by the monarchs of Spain. Most of these appointees were tyrants, but there were a few capable rulers who worked earnestly for the good of their subjects. During this same period, Colombia's Indian population declined, mostly because of harsh treatment at the hands of the Spaniards and because of diseases introduced to the New World by the Europeans. To make up for this loss of labor, enslaved Africans were introduced to cultivate farms and to work in the mines. Despite extraordinary hardships, blacks slowly increased in number.

Within Colombia the Spanish established an unjust system of land use through two institutions. The first institution was the encomienda under which the Spanish crown granted land—complete with Indian laborers—to Spanish land-owners. The new landowners were, in turn, responsible for Christianizing the workers and for making a profit from agriculture. Indians were thus forced to work as serfs on lands they formerly had occupied as free people. The second organized means of exploitation was the plantation system. The encomienda system lasted until about 1700, by which time most encomiendas had been returned to the crown, and only a few new ones were granted. The plantation system remained in force until the abolition of slavery in 1851. The legacy of that institution is still evident in some areas of Colombia, where blacks continue to experience discrimination.

Remote from the seat of Spanish power, Colombia developed on its own. There were skirmishes with the Indians, power struggles between Church and civil authorities, and a growing division between the territory's foreign-born exploiters and the rising generation of New World Colombians. Many Colombians died from diseases such as malaria, smallpox, typhoid, and dysentery. As settlements grew in size and economic importance, Colombians complained about the lack of roads and schools.

Piracy

As further evidence of Spain's neglect of the colony, Colombia's defenses were weak. Territorial forces were often unable to defend Colombian ports from raiding pirate ships flying the colors of Spain's Old World rivals, such as France and Great Britain.

The vast amounts of gold, silver, and precious stones that Spain was harvesting from its New World colonies resulted in frequent acts of piracy. A decree from Spain declared that treasure-laden ships should return home in groups to avoid assault. The vessels gathered at designated ports—such as Cartagena in present-day northern Colombia—all of which eventually were fortified heavily. The expense of protecting the ports is illustrated by the legendary story that King

Courtesy of Museum of Modern Art of Latin America

The fortress of San Felipe de Barajas was built by slaves from 1630 to 1657 to protect Cartagena from attack from the sea. The thick walls of the fortress conceal an underground network of passageways, with soldiers' quarters, storerooms, and tunnels—spaces where enough arms and supplies could be housed to make the fortress self-sufficient for months.

Philip II—who provided the money for the barricades—once looked out from his palace window in Spain saying, "I am looking for the walls of Cartagena. They cost so much, they must be visible from here."

Sir Francis Drake, the English buccaneer and explorer, harassed Cartagena in 1586 and proved he could get through the port's defenses. In 1697 Baron de Pointis and 10,000 French troops captured Cartagena, took nine-tenths of the wealth in the town, and returned to a hero's welcome in France.

Creole Discontent

Divisions, which were aired by increasingly outspoken Church and civil officials, appeared in New Granada between rulers and ruled. The main disagreement cen-

England's Sir Francis Drake easily got through the defenses at Cartagena in the sixteenth century, after which the Spanish authorities further strengthened the port's fortifications.

tered on a Spanish system that reserved for the Spanish-born the highest positions in all realms of life. Those of Spanish bloodlines born in the New World—called criollos, or Creoles—were accorded lower-ranking jobs. Their discontent with this situation was a primary cause of the 1781 Rebellion of the Comuneros (townspeople).

The number of anticolonials increased as Colombians became better educated, thanks to the success of local efforts to modernize public education. New institutions of higher learning were established, which helped prepare Colombians for independence. Antonio Nariño, for example, may have lived to regret his Spanish translation of the French work, *Declaration of the Rights of Man and Citizen,* which brought him exile and arrest for its ideas of equality. But the work established him firmly among the forebears of Colombian independence.

Between 1785 and 1810 discontent among the colony's Creoles grew into a political movement aimed at forcing overdue changes in colonial policy. The group sought

A New World coin was minted in 1756 and carries the royal coat of arms of the Bourbon monarchs of Spain.

Bolívar and his troops crossed the Andes from Venezuela in the rainy season to arrive in Colombian territory in 1819. Here, "the Liberator"—as Bolívar is sometimes called—prepares his troops to cross the Páramo de Pisba before the Battle of Boyacá.

greater local self-government and the abolition of restrictions on the colony's trade. When Napoleon's forces invaded Spain, leaders in Bogotá decided to take advantage of Spain's weakness and issued the Act of Independence on July 20, 1810 —which today is celebrated as Independence Day in Colombia. While it pledged the colony's continued loyalty to the Spanish crown and to the exiled king Ferdinand VII, this act provided for more local self-government within the colony.

Several years of confused lines of authority followed as local revolutionary leaders squabbled among themselves about the design of the new system of government. Taking advantage of differences of opinion within the self-declared independent colony, Spain reestablished its control over the territory in 1814. Colombian revolutionary forces fled to the eastern plains where they regrouped under the leadership of Francisco de Paula Santander. These Colombians later joined the forces of Simon Bolívar, a Venezuelan patriot, in the Orinoco Valley, and on August 7, 1819,

the combined army defeated the Spanish forces at the Battle of Boyacá.

Following the establishment of a provisional government, a constitutional convention met at Ciudad Bolívar in Venezuela. Colombia's first constitution was finally adopted at Cúcuta in 1821. Bolívar left General Santander in charge at Bogotá and pressed southward with his forces of South American liberation. Colombia's story as a nation thus began as part of a union comprising the territories of present-day Venezuela, Ecuador, Peru, Bolivia, Panama, and Colombia.

Independence

Santander proved to be an able leader, who helped to balance Church-state relations, to improve public education, and to bring about economic order. While the country prospered, its citizens separated into factions from which Colombia's two present political parties—the Conservatives and the Liberals—developed. The Conservatives leaned toward limited voting rights,

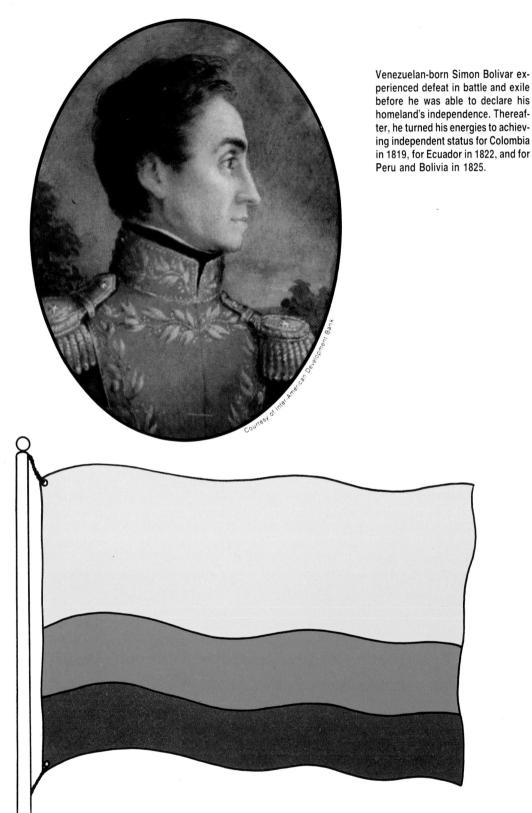

Venezuelan-born Simon Bolívar experienced defeat in battle and exile before he was able to declare his homeland's independence. Thereafter, he turned his energies to achieving independent status for Colombia in 1819, for Ecuador in 1822, and for Peru and Bolivia in 1825.

Courtesy of Inter-American Development Bank

Artwork by Jim Simondet

In designing their national flag, Colombians adopted the same colors that were used by Simon Bolívar for the flag of Gran Colombia—the federation of the freed colonial territories of Venezuela, Ecuador, Peru, Bolivia, Panama, and Colombia.

The Roman Catholic cathedral in Bogotá stands in Plaza Bolívar—the heart of the capital. Colombia's political ties to the Church continued to be strong after independence and through much of the twentieth century.

centralized government, colonial-era privileges, and strong Church-state ties. The Liberals advocated federalized government, extension of voting rights, and separation of Church and state.

The nineteenth century was marred by uprisings, civil wars, and short-lived constitutions. The power of the Church was reduced, and much of its property was taken away. Elected president as a Liberal, poet Rafael Núñez gradually leaned more toward traditionally Conservative views. His Constitution of 1886, which made Catholicism the state religion, was hardly changed at all until 1936. Ruling like a dictator until his death in 1894, Núñez helped to restore central government, abolish local sovereignty, and return Church power. The results were peace and order at the price of little economic growth and of individual freedoms. Soon after Núñez's death, a violent revolution, the War of a Thousand Days, broke out in Colombia.

Over 100,000 people were killed, and the country was reduced to economic ruin.

The Twentieth Century

During the 1880s Colombia had granted rights to a French company—La Compagnie Universelle du Canale Interocéanique de Panama—to dig a canal across the Isthmus of Panama. This project failed, and the French sold their rights to the United States. When the Colombian congress refused to ratify a 1903 treaty giving the United States permission to build the canal, a group of residents of the isthmus—with assurance of protection from the United States—declared Panama's independence from Colombia. By strictly fulfilling an earlier commitment to protect the Panama Railroad, the United States prevented Colombian troops from getting to Panama City in order to stop the independence movement. U.S. President

Even before Panama declared its independence from Colombia, some preliminary work had already begun on the construction of the Panama Canal. Here a steam shovel clears rock from what will become Gaillard Cut.

Theodore Roosevelt recognized the new country immediately and signed a treaty with it to build the canal.

The loss of Panama caused strains in U.S.-Colombia relations. The U.S. Congress awarded Colombia $25 million in 1931 to compensate for its loss, but ill feelings still existed.

During the first half of the twentieth century, Colombia's two political parties competed for control of the government. The prestige of Liberal president Alfonso López Pumarejo was enhanced by his role in settling a border conflict with Peru to Colombia's advantage. This improved standing enabled him to initiate a major social reform program. Bills were passed that benefited workers, increased the taxes of the rich, and provided a public education system free of Church control. In 1936 a new constitution was drafted providing for the separation of Church and state and declaring public welfare a governmental function.

When López Pumarejo was elected to a second term as president in 1942—following an interval in which the reforms he had instituted gained strength—Conservatives were not at all happy. Moreover, López Pumarejo himself was caught between the crossfire of his own party's left and right wings. There were increasingly bitter strikes by workers whose expectations had been raised. The president's program was blocked in Colombia's congress by the alliance of his own party's right wing with opponents on the Conservative side. Uncontrollable inflation set in, and scandals

After the murder of Gaitán, Carlos Lleras Restrepo became one of the most active critics of Presidents Ospina Pérez and Gómez.

La Violencia lasted for 10 years and drove thousands of rural Colombians from their homes to seek the safety of the cities. The physical growth of Medellín—along with its population explosion—can partially be traced to this decade of countrywide warfare during the 1950s.

were revealed in the administration. Extremist Conservatives—who sided with the Axis powers of Germany, Italy, and Japan in World War II—were outraged when Colombia declared war on the side of the Allies in 1943.

Finally, López Pumarejo was forced to resign, after having suffered the humiliation of seeing himself and his cabinet held prisoner by the Colombian army. In 1945 he was succeeded in office by Alberto Lleras Camargo, but neither Lleras Camargo nor his successor, Mariano Ospina Pérez of the Conservative party, was able to head off a growing tension that was soon to burst forth in bloodshed.

La Violencia

The main event that sparked La Violencia was the 1948 assassination in Bogotá of Jorge Eliécer Gaitán, a popular Liberal leader. In the ensuing days of violence, Bogotá was rendered a shambles as mobs engaged in uncontrolled destruction.

Violence soon engulfed all of Bogotá and left 1,500 Bogotaños dead. But the prolonged fighting, which was rooted in age-old political rivalries between the Conservative and Liberal parties, took place in the countryside, too. Rural people were as frightened by the rise in violence as they were by the killing of Gaitán. During the next 10 years, some 200,000 Colombians were killed. Some of those involved were politically motivated, while others were bandits, who took advantage of the unsettled conditions to raid and loot. Hundreds of thousands of Colombians streamed into the nation's large cities, where authorities concentrated all available forces on restoring order.

From this period of lawlessness, a repressive dictatorship emerged, led by Laureano Gómez Castro and later by Gustavo Rojas Pinilla. By 1958 the dictatorship had run its course, Rojas was exiled, and Colombians vowed that such a cruel sequence of events must never occur again. Differences between Liberal and

Lieutenant General Gustavo Rojas Pinilla, Colombia's last dictator, was forced out of office in 1957.

Conservative parties, which had brought about the violent nightmare in the first place, had to yield to compromise if future anarchy was to be avoided. The spirit of this public agreement was contained in a pair of documents—the Pact of Benidorm and the Declaration of Sitges—which were worked out by former presidents Lleras Camargo and Gómez.

Colombians confirmed the arrangement, eventually dubbed the National Front, through a popular vote. Colombia's Conservative and Liberal parties agreed to rotate the presidency for the next 16 years. Each four-year administration pledged to rule over what amounted to a coalition government, and high offices were to be shared by both parties. The National Front worked so well it was extended until 1986. That year, amid general agreement that democracy had taken deep root in Colombia, president-elect Virgilio Bar-

co appointed members of his party to positions in high offices.

As elsewhere in Latin America in recent years, Colombia has seen the emergence of armed guerrillas, who are anxious to achieve necessary reforms—most notably in the area of equal distribution of wealth. Successive administrations have offered the guerrillas a general pardon and an opportunity to participate in the Colombian democratic process in return for laying down their arms. One sizable guerrilla faction—the Colombian Revolutionary Armed Forces—accepted the offer in 1985 but in 1987 began arming itself again.

The legacy of La Violencia continues not only in the antigovernment guerrilla movements but also in the heightened violence

Alberto Lleras Camargo was one of the chief architects of modern Colombian democracy and twice served as president of the country.

During his four-year term (1986–1990), President Virgilio Barco took a strong stance against the international problem of drug trafficking, which is centered in Colombia. In addition, he was compelled to confront many internal social problems.

Courtesy of Embassy of Colombia, Washington, D.C.

surrounding the illegal drug traffic. Drug cartel leaders have large sums of money with which to bribe judges, government employees, and police officials. These corrupted individuals inform the drug lords of any attempts to destroy their operations. Assassins are hired to kill uncooperative and influential citizens. Despite attempts on the lives of politicians, the May 1990 presidential election is not expected to be postponed.

Government

Colombia is a democratic republic with a centralized government and separate executive, legislative, and judicial branches.

The president is elected by direct vote for a four-year term and cannot serve more than one term in succession. If a president resigns or dies and less than two years of the term remain, the legislative body elects a substitute president to serve out the remaining period. If more than two years remain, the substitute president must call for new elections. The president appoints a cabinet of 13 ministers and is aided in decision making by a 10-member council of state.

The legislative body consists of a bicameral (two-house) congress. Each department (state) of the nation is represented by two senators plus one additional senator for every 200,000 people. There are also two representatives for each department plus one more for every 100,000 people.

Members of the Supreme Court rule on all constitutional questions and serve as the final court of appeal. Justices are elected by the congress from nominations made by the president and are reappointed every five years.

Providing proper schooling at the primary level remains a problem for Colombian authorities. These children—from families that have settled on newly opened farmland—lack school facilities.

3) The People

Because of rapid urbanization, Colombia has undergone deep and sometimes traumatic changes in recent years. More than two-thirds of the country's 31.2 million people live in cities, compared to less than one-third of the population 30 years ago.

In the process of becoming a nation of urbanites, Colombians have experienced the breakup of old family and village patterns of living.

Urbanization

The pace of urbanization has been so rapid that Colombian authorities have fallen far behind in their efforts to provide jobs, housing, and schooling for all those who have settled in the cities. Before the rush to move to the city, urban life was quiet and simple; since the population explosion, however, city life has deteriorated markedly. Sprawling slums have become breeding grounds for crime that endangers the citizens of most Colombian cities.

Many urban newcomers lack skills and cannot find good jobs. The prices for available real estate have skyrocketed. Even with two members of a family holding jobs, it is still difficult to afford the often high monthly cost of renting an apartment.

Colombian municipal and federal authorities have tried many schemes for meeting their obligations to the people. Some primary and secondary schools are operated on double shifts, with two sets of students using the same classrooms in a single day. Some cities, unable to accommodate the influx of new people, have bulldozed tracts of land and opened them up to newcomers

Rapid urbanization has been felt most keenly in Bogotá, where there are not enough jobs – or enough land – to support the new arrivals.

on a first-come, first-served basis. These recently arrived families construct make-shift homes, which they gradually improve as they earn money.

Ethnic Origins

Mestizos (people of mixed Indian-and-European bloodlines) make up almost 50 percent of Colombia's population. Those of

35

pure European (mainly Spanish) ancestry comprise about 20 percent. At the bottom of the economic ladder are the zambos of mixed black-and-Indian stock, who make up 23 percent of the population; the blacks, with 6 percent; and the pure Indians, who represent only 1 percent.

Colombia's blacks and zambos are concentrated mainly in the lowlands, including port cities on both the Atlantic and Pacific oceans. While Colombians may pride themselves on being free of racial prejudice, there is no doubt that blacks and zambos historically have been the victims of governmental neglect and discrimination. Few blacks or zambos have become prominent on the national scene, and Colombians consider the living condition of blacks in the port of Buenaventura to be a national disgrace.

Independent Picture Service

Colombians perform a ceremonial **dance.**

Regionalism

As might be expected from its varied geography and the diverse origins of its people, Colombia remains a nation with marked regional differences. The pace of life in the highlands, especially in Andean

Courtesy of Inter-American Development Bank

The slums around Buenaventura — such as Barrio Muro Yusti — are considered among the worst in Latin America. Wooden shacks built over the water lack sewage facilities, with the result that all waste is dumped in the surrounding waters.

Regionalism is manifested in Colombia's avid interest in bullfighting – a sport imported with the Spanish conquistadors. The bullring in Bogotá is modeled after one in Madrid.

Even the means of transportation are affected by regionalism. Indians of the Amazon lowlands travel in canoes made from hollowed-out logs.

cities, is much faster than in the lowlands or along the coasts. People dress differently for their distinctive climates, have developed eating preferences peculiar to their region's agricultural production, and tend to be somewhat suspicious of Colombians from other areas.

Regionalism is evident in music and dance, cultural heritage, and outlook on life. It also extends to politics, to economics—with each region demanding the development of its own particular resources —and to hard-fought competition on the sports fields.

The departments of Colombia were laid out to enhance regional attributes. Public education has been placed largely under local administration. Each Colombian de-partment is fiercely proud of its own style of living and its cultural achievements.

Religion

The Roman Catholic hierarchy probably has more influence in Colombia than in any other South American country. There are few people more steadfast in the practice of their religion than Colombians.

While freedom of worship is guaranteed in the constitution, the law is not always strictly enforced. In 1957 an amendment confirmed that Roman Catholicism was to be the national religion. The state pledged to "protect the Church and make it respected as a necessary element of social order." Other religions were to be "allowed

Photo by Dr. Roma Hoff

Cartagena's cathedral was begun in 1575 and came under attack during Drake's raid in 1586. The cathedral was completed in the early seventeenth century.

Music plays an important role in all aspects of Indian life. Here, singers march in a village funeral procession.

as long as they were not contrary to Christian morals or the law." On the whole Protestant missions in rural areas have been unsuccessful and often meet with opposition by the people.

According to the Colombian constitution, courses in Roman Catholicism are required in public schools, and the curriculum must not conflict with Church teachings. While the Church is not directly in control of public education, only private schools have complete freedom. As in other parts of the world, however, social change has begun to modify the Church's traditional conservative position.

Music

Bogotá supports both a national conservatory and a national symphony orchestra. Concerts and operas are performed regularly in the ornate Colón Theater across the street from the national palace.

Colombian music combines the melancholy spirit of the Andes with the rhythmic African vitality of the lowlands. There are work songs (*zabrás*), marching songs (*guabinas* and *torbellinos*), religious songs (*gualies*, *albados*, and *trisagios*), and ballads called *coplas,* which describe certain events or emotions. The funeral of a child is solemnized by the singing of a *chigualo.* Traditional Indian music often can be heard along the southern and eastern rivers. A black spiritual melody, called the *currulao,* is frequently sung at baptisms, weddings, and corn harvests.

Festivals

One of Colombia's most popular regional celebrations is the pre-Lenten Carnival in Barranquilla, with its parade of floats,

The rhythmic *cumbia* is an African dance that is very popular with Colombians who live on the Caribbean coast.

masquerades, and dance contests. Cartagena commemorates its independence from Spain in a similar manner, with fireworks, serenades, and dancing accompanied by maracas and hurdy-gurdy players. A coffee queen is selected at the January Manizales Fair, in the course of festivities such as bullfights, folk dancing, and international sports competitions.

Among major religious festivals is San Juan's Day (June 24), when people eat, drink, dance, and watch bullfights in the town squares of Tolima department. On San Pedro's Day (June 29), there is also feasting, dancing, copla singing, and a tournament on horseback in which riders try to behead a symbolic animal hanging from a crossbar.

The festival of Colombia's national patron, the Virgin Mary of the Rosary of Chinquinquira, is one of the most famous in the Americas. Each year on October 7, thousands of pilgrims come to celebrate this solemn religious ceremony.

Ceremonies in Popayán during the week before Easter are an authentic display of

Blacks are Colombia's most-neglected economic group. Many people collect their water from public taps to avoid health hazards caused by lack of pure drinking water.

old Spanish tradition in Colombia. On this occasion, traditional Christian rites are carried out in the same manner as they have been for almost 400 years.

Language and Education

Spanish is Colombia's official language. The Spanish written and spoken by educated people in Bogotá and Popayán is considered by some to be the purest in Latin America. The only people who do not speak Spanish are the small percentage of pure Indians who live in remote regions of the Andes. Among the Indian groups who have retained a great many of their own words and customs are the Arhuacos of the Sierra Nevada, the Motilón of the Orinoco Valley, and some natives of the Chocó region and La Guajira Peninsula.

Although illiteracy has dropped over 50 percent in the last 60 years, there is still much to be done in the field of education. More than 20 percent of the population over the age of 20 has had no schooling at all. About 80 percent of the people are considered literate.

Primary education in Colombia is free and compulsory, but facilities are limited. About 33,000 primary schools enroll just over four million pupils, and almost two million students attend the 5,000 secondary schools. Institutions of higher education enroll more than 365,000 students. The National University in Bogotá was founded in 1867, and there are 97 other universities.

Health

Standards of public health are low in Colombia, and medical facilities are still inadequate, especially in rural areas. Physicians practice mainly in the metropolitan

Courtesy of World Bank

At a high school in Medellín, students take their work seriously. Colombia's education system is slowly changing its focus to include vocational and technical training at the secondary level. This new system will better prepare the students to fill the country's need for skilled labor in business, industry, and agriculture.

areas, and, consequently, rural regions—such as those in and around Buenaventura—suffer grave shortages of trained medical personnel. Life expectancy at birth is 64 years, and the infant mortality rate is 46 deaths in every 1,000 live births.

Malnutrition is a frequent problem in the countryside. Babies often die from easily treatable forms of dysentery or from nutritional diseases—such as, scurvy (caused by lack of Vitamin C) and anemia (iron-poor blood). Venereal and respiratory diseases are also common, as is the threat of infections, such as yellow fever, caused by insects in slums that lack proper sewage and water systems. The chewing of coca leaves (from which cocaine is processed) and an increase in the use of cocaine among Colombians take a further toll on the health of the nation's population. Coca-leaf chewing is said to dull sensations of hunger and cold.

Buenaventura's slums lack nearly every amenity—from proper sewage facilities to doctors.

Coca is a South American shrub that grows from three to six feet high. The dried leaves contain cocaine and are made into a paste for further processing into a fine, white powder.

The market in the village of Choachí, near Bogotá, springs to life every week and displays the variety of homegrown vegetables and fruits available in the area.

Photo by Amandus Schneider

Food

Colombia's food is rich and highly seasoned. Given the nation's diverse terrain, there are also regional dishes, which draw on the country's varied crops. *Ajiaco,* a Bogotá specialty, is a spicy soup made of potatoes, chicken, capers, ears of corn, and avocados. The high-quality native beef is used in making empanadas—pancakes rolled into a cone, stuffed with finely chopped meat and vegetables, and topped with chili sauce. A Cartagena specialty is *arroz con coco,* rice sauteed with fresh coconut. In Tolima a favorite dish is *viuda de pescado* (literally, fish widow), which consists of cabbage greens stuffed with fish and baked in a pit lined and covered with banana leaves. Coffee, of course, is the national drink. Other beverages are chicha (maize beer) and aguardiente (licorice brandy).

Journalism

Newspapers are powerful organs of public opinion in Colombia. Almost every town publishes at least one daily paper, from rough, hand-printed sheets in small towns to large, national dailies. Thirty-one dailies have a circulation of 1.5 million. *El Tiempo* and *El Espectador* are Liberal papers published in Bogotá. *La República* and *El Siglo* express Conservative viewpoints.

The constitution provides that the press shall be free in time of peace but "responsible in accordance with the law when it may attack personal reputation, the social order, or public tranquillity." Although censorship has occurred during times of national emergency, a high level of journalistic freedom and responsibility has been maintained in the country. The Colombian press recently has united to protest in print the incidences of drug-related violence throughout the nation. The journals have also begun to expose and question the amount of high-level corruption in government caused by connections to the drug trade.

Photo by Don Irish

A statue of author Jorge Isaacs and of characters from his work *María* stands in Cali's civic center.

Courtesy of U.S. Drug Enforcement Administration

Journalists in Colombia have come out strongly against the illicit drug trade. At this remote shelter in the jungle, neatly packaged marijuana is ready for export to the United States. The illegal drug will be carried aboard airplanes flying out of rough jungle airstrips to land at secret locations in the southern United States.

Literature

Colombian writers have exercised great influence on national life. In 1982 the Nobel Prize for literature was awarded to Gabriel García Márquez for his remarkable tales of Latin America, which unite fantasy and realism. Jorge Isaacs's *María* (1867) is a popular novel of love and death in rural Colombia, while José Eustacio Rivera's *La Vorágine* (The vortex) describes social rebellion in the twentieth century.

José Asunción Silva is an outstanding poet whose *Nocturnos* is considered one of the finest poems in the Spanish language. Other noted poets are romanticist José Eusebio Caro and Julio Arboleda, who is the author of the national epic, *Gonzalo de Oyón*. More poets than soldiers have served as president of Colombia.

A detail from a painting entitled *A Lady* by Fernando Botero reveals his characteristic style—well-rounded and puffy figures, who oftentimes are depicted in a way that pokes fun at society.

Fine and Folk Arts

Traditions in the fine arts have long been influenced in Colombia by trends established elsewhere in the world. In colonial times this meant that Colombian artists and builders extended and interpreted art forms based on far-away European models. In modern times many Colombian artists have been as at home in New York and Paris, as in Bogotá, and works produced in Colombia have reflected an internationalist spirit.

Typical of this tradition is Fernando Botero, who was born in Medellín in 1932. He and his early paintings found a cool reception in the art circles of Bogotá. Botero eventually earned his reputation after settling in New York City in 1960. Today he is considered perhaps the foremost Colombian painter of the twentieth century, and his works now adorn the walls of galleries at home and abroad.

In addition, within Colombia there is a remarkable skill in the production of handicrafts, an art form called *artes populares* that is a part of everyday life. Many Colombians are extremely gifted as craftspeople and fashion decorative objects,

An Indian demonstrates the great precision used in the production of carved *artes populares* (popular art).

tools, and household items of such varied materials as glass, metal, ceramics, and textiles.

Boat on the Magdalena River is a primitive-style painting by Noé León, an artist who began his career selling small paintings to people on the streets of Barranquilla.

The colors are rich, varied, and bold in this painting entitled *Tiger in the Jungle* by Noé León.

Before dawn the wholesale market in Medellín becomes a busy place. Approximately 2,000 tons of produce are handled here daily—evidence of Colombia's expanding range of agricultural production.

4) The Economy

In recent years Colombia's economy has undergone a change, with the country today producing a constantly expanding range of agricultural, mining, and manufactured products. The transition has caused severe hardships for many Colombians, particularly immigrants to the cities from rural areas who lack industrial skills.

Employment

Officially, unemployment stands at roughly 14.5 percent of those who are able to work. Unofficially, however, sources estimate unemployment and underemployment at nearly one-quarter of those who

are able to work. In trying to cope with the problem of retraining its citizens for jobs in modern industry, the Colombian government has developed one of the most comprehensive and far-reaching programs of vocational education in Latin America.

Training in needed job skills is now built into the country's public education system. There are night courses for Colombians who are already employed but who wish to advance by learning new skills. Young urban residents flock to schools offering training in computers and computer programming.

Colombia's cities have established non-profit programs, which provide business

A new school at Barranquilla provides instruction for high school students in vocational, agricultural, and business subjects to prepare them with the skills to obtain jobs. The curriculum represents a departure from past patterns of education, which focused exclusively on preparing high school students for entry into colleges and universities.

training to very small enterprises. These businesses produce goods and services in poor neighborhoods where there are few large firms geared to the needs of poor people. Through this training, owners of small, home-based businesses are more capable of expanding their production. Moreover, they are encouraged to register their businesses legally in order to make their enterprises eligible for established sources of credit—from banks and other financial institutions. Through experience in these programs, urban Colombians have learned that an amazing proportion of their nation's business is accomplished informally, through a vigorous and dynamic underground economy.

Economic Growth

Today less than one third of Colombia's work force is engaged in agriculture.

An Indian woman's production of handwoven cloth is a good example of Colombia's thriving underground economy.

48

The business cooperative to which Margarita de Bernal belongs received a loan of about $325 from Artesanías de Colombia to purchase more leather to increase its production of goods. Fourteen people belong to this Bogotá cooperative—called El Encanto—and produce a variety of handmade leather items.

Tailor Argemiro Cárdenas received an $800 loan from Fundación Carvajal, a Cali-based nonprofit organization that provides economic assistance to low-income groups. Señor Cárdenas purchased a new cloth cutter, which he believed would increase his production by 20 percent.

49

Colombia's mountainous terrain has hampered development throughout the country.

Between 1965 and 1986, this percentage declined from 45 to 26 percent. Nearly 20 percent of the nation's workers are involved in manufacturing, and the country's mining production has been growing in value by about 25 percent a year. The latter figure reflects the profits of huge new investments in the development of extensive coal resources in northern Colombia.

Among the factors handicapping Colombia's economic growth are difficulties posed by the country's mountainous terrain and by unsettled political conditions in rural areas due to conflicts between guerrilla groups and government forces. The government has undertaken extraordinary efforts to compromise with rebel elements, but violence still delays development of the countryside.

Colombia and Illegal Drugs

An area of economic growth that the government hopes to curtail is the cultivation and processing of illegal drugs. Colombian authorities have seized hundreds of luxurious homes and other possessions of suspected drug traffickers. To reclaim their property, they must appear in person and prove that they acquired their goods with money earned legally. Raids on cocaine factories have increased. Arrested traffickers face being extradited (sent to another country to face charges and stand trial) to the United States. The drug lords have declared they would rather die in Colombia than live in a U.S. prison.

The cartels fight back with death threats. Especially vulnerable are judges and journalists who do not accept the bribes of the traffickers. The outspoken Bogotá newspaper *El Espectator* has been a target because of its stance against illegal drug operations. Several of the newspaper's employees have been assassinated, and part of its head office has been bombed.

The introduction of huge sums of money into the Colombian economy through this illegal source has made it difficult for elected authorities to control financial matters. Uncounted and unaccounted for money has boosted inflation—since people have untaxable money to spend—and has caused a rise in crime. On a judicial level narcotics cases have become dangerous to decide. Several judges handling such cases have been killed in gangland violence.

In Colombia's dry La Guajira Peninsula, acres of high-priced marijuana plants ripen in the sun. Most of the crop will be sold to dealers who operate in the United States —taking advantage of a widespread and illegal North American indulgence. At one time, Mexico supplied most of the U.S. dope, but effective herbicides curbed Mexican production. Farmers in Colombia gladly filled the demand, though the government in Bogotá is also authorizing the use of herbicides to kill marijuana plants. Colombia now supplies about half of all the marijuana purchased in the United States.

Colombia's drug connection—the so-called Medellín cartel—has knitted together a

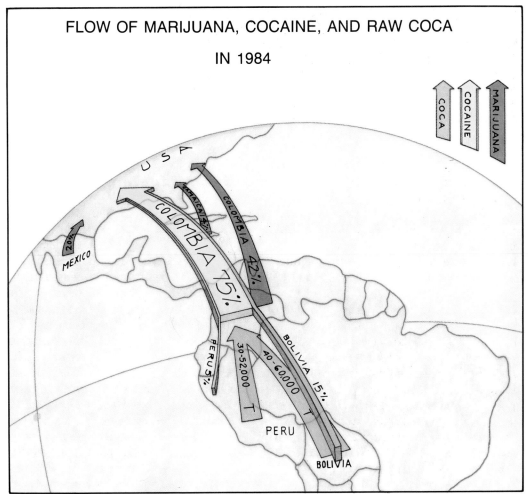

Artwork by Carol F. Barrett

This chart shows the country of origin and the percentage of total U.S. supplies of marijuana and cocaine that are sent to the United States from Latin America. Although coca is cultivated in Colombia itself, the chart also illustrates the movement of tonnages of Bolivian and Peruvian coca to Colombia for processing into cocaine. (Data from *Narcotics Intelligence Estimate 1984* compiled by the U.S. Drug Enforcement Administration, Washington, D.C.)

A remote location on Colombia's Caribbean coast is among the many places used by drug traffickers to export marijuana and processed cocaine to the United States.

network of farmers, producers, brokers, and dealers stretching from Medellín and Bogotá to New York, Chicago, and Los Angeles. Well-known traffickers—such as Pablo Escobar Gaviria, Jorge Luis Ochoa, and José Gonzalo Rodríguez Gacha—own ships and planes and employ pilots, electronics experts, and thugs. They have made their illegal and dangerous enterprise one of the largest businesses in Colombia.

Reputedly, 80 percent of the cocaine used in the United States comes through the Colombian network, though much of the coca is grown elsewhere—in Peru and Bolivia. Why has Colombia become the leader in the drug field? Perhaps because the soil in the Andean area of Colombia is ideal for the cultivation of marijuana. Possibly because La Guajira Peninsula on the Caribbean coast of Colombia is a smuggler's—and a drug trafficker's—dream. It is isolated, badly patrolled, and full of tiny inlets and bays well suited to secret drug pickups. Likely, too, is the notion that Colombia's period of La Violencia gave these frontier areas—far removed from Bogotá —their own kind of rough justice. Worse still is that growing marijuana illegally is more profitable for local Colombian farmers than growing legitimate crops, such as coffee, corn, or cotton.

Colombia's military—after much foot dragging due to widespread corruption— has slowly begun to crack down on small, makeshift airstrips used for drug running. They have also begun to disrupt the production and distribution of processed drugs to the United States. But as former Colombian president Julio César Turbay Ayala said about U.S. users of illegal narcotics, "If you abandon illegal drugs, the traffic will disappear."

Agriculture and Livestock

With its diverse topography and climate, Colombia can produce a wide range of crops varying from those that require warm temperatures—such as bananas—to those that prefer cooler climates—such as potatoes. Many highland farms are small, however, and their owners cling to traditional subsistence crops and employ simple methods of agriculture. In areas where the land is more level and where the use of modern techniques is less costly, irrigation and new chemical fertilizers are used.

Surprisingly, only 5 percent of Colombia's arable land is under cultivation. Six million acres are described as fit for crops, and 96 million acres are believed usable as pastureland.

Coffee remains the nation's chief agricultural product, and Colombia is the world's second largest producer, after Brazil. Coffee beans grow best at an elevation of between 4,300 and 6,600 feet; the heaviest concentration of shrubs in Colombia is near Medellín. Most coffee farms have small acreages.

Sugarcane is cultivated throughout the hot and temperate areas of the country, especially on the central Pacific coast in the Cauca River Valley. The cane is mostly made into unrefined brown sugar; some of it is refined into sugar, molasses, or alco-

Independent Picture Service

Coffee-bean picking is a time-consuming job done by hand. Through long experience, workers have learned to choose only the ripest beans.

hol. Bananas—an important export—are grown along the Caribbean coast. Maize thrives under most climatic conditions,

Courtesy of United Nations

Andean Indians of the Cauca Valley weed a field in preparation for planting potatoes.

Maize thrives at many elevations and is an important part of the Colombian diet.

except at the highest elevations, and is a food staple, especially for the poor. Rice production is increasing, particularly in hot and humid regions. Other crops important either in acreage or in amount produced include cotton, potatoes, manioc, wheat, barley, tobacco, cacao, and beans.

Colombia has become one of the principal livestock-producing countries in South America. In the early 1980s the cattle population was estimated at over 26 million, giving the country almost as many cows as people. Most of the stock is raised in the Sinú and San Jorge river valleys and the eastern llanos. High-quality animals are raised in the Cundinamarca Basin, outside of Bogotá, and in the valleys of the Cauca and Sinú rivers. Other livestock include horses, mules, donkeys, pigs, sheep,

Horses graze on many Colombian hillsides. Today over half of the acreage of Colombian farms is used as pastureland.

Photo by Dr. Roma Hoff

A ranch hand wears a ruana, or cape, as he herds animals into a corral at the Medellín market.

Courtesy of Inter-American Development Bank

In Boyacá department, a technician from Colombia's Ministry of Agriculture demonstrates how to administer medicine to a sick sheep—through a tube inserted down the animal's throat.

55

Courtesy of Inter-American Development Bank

Grain storage silos figure in a view of Santa Marta—the principal Colombian port on the Caribbean.

and goats. Poultry raising has expanded greatly due to the use of modern production techniques.

Trade

As Colombia's leading trade partner, the United States buys most of Colombia's exports and supplies most of its imports. Trade is also carried on with Venezuela, Japan, Germany, Brazil, and the Netherlands. The country's strategic location near the Panama Canal, which connects the Pacific and Atlantic oceans, gives Colombia contact with leading world markets. Furthermore, the tributaries of the Amazon and Orinoco rivers that border Colombia also provide access to trade. The most important seaports are Cartagena, Santa Marta, and Barranquilla on the Caribbean Sea and Buenaventura on the Pacific Ocean.

Principal legal exports are coffee, bananas, flowers, sugar, clothing, and textiles. Marijuana and cocaine are exported illegally, and these exports may even earn the most income. Leading imports are machinery, vehicles, tractors, metals, rubber, chemical products, wheat, fertilizers, and wool.

Trade Unions

The Colombian constitution guarantees workers the right to strike if they agree to lawful requirements. While all plants and mines are unionized, only one-tenth of the workers belong to unions. The National Union of Colombian Workers, established by the Jesuit religious order in 1946, is conservative. The Confederation of Colombian Workers, formed in 1935, is an independent organization.

Legislation guarantees paid sick leave, overtime rates, paid vacations, maximum working hours, health and accident insurance, and severance pay (money given to an employee upon the ending of employment) for all workers. Many large

Thousands of bananas from the countryside surrounding Santa Marta wait to be loaded on export ships.

Coffee sacks sit on the docks at Buenaventura—Colombia's busiest Pacific port. It handles 80 percent of the nation's coffee exports and 60 percent of all exports combined.

corporations maintain primary schools for their employees' children and pay retirement pensions to people over 55 years old who have been with the company more than 20 years.

Industry

Colombian industry expanded rapidly after 1930 when a protective tariff was adopted. In 1941 the government organized an industrial development board to encourage certain industries that would later be allowed to move into private hands after the industries had proven to be successful. In 1950 a large, government-owned steel mill was built at Paz de Río in Boyacá department.

Textile factories contribute greatly to the national income and employ a large percentage of workers. Woven products are of good quality and are exported, in addition to supplying local demand. The Instituto de Fomento Industrial (IFI, Institute of Industrial Development) loans

Courtesy of Inter-American Development Bank

A field hand displays a giant yucca plant that was specially developed for commercial use in making starch. Although too acidic for human consumption, this variety of yucca also can be transformed into animal feed.

Courtesy of Inter-American Development Bank

A worker operates a Swiss-manufactured, automatic weaving machine at FABRICATO, a huge textile factory located in Medellín. The company also has automated indigo dying machines, which color the thread used in making blue jeans.

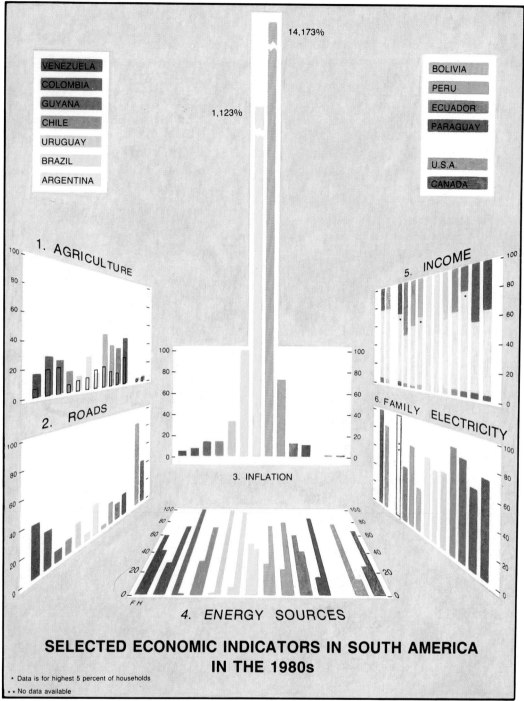

VENEZUELA
COLOMBIA
GUYANA
CHILE
URUGUAY
BRAZIL
ARGENTINA

BOLIVIA
PERU
ECUADOR
PARAGUAY

U.S.A.
CANADA

14,173%

1,123%

1. AGRICULTURE

5. INCOME

2. ROADS

6. FAMILY ELECTRICITY

3. INFLATION

4. ENERGY SOURCES

**SELECTED ECONOMIC INDICATORS IN SOUTH AMERICA
IN THE 1980s**

* Data is for highest 5 percent of households

** No data available

Artwork by Carol F. Barrett

This multigraph depicts six important South American economic factors. The same factors for the United States and Canada are included for comparison. Data is from *1986 Britannica Book of the Year, Encyclopedia of the Third World, Europa Yearbook,* and *Countries of the World and their Leaders, 1987.*

In GRAPH 1—labeled Agriculture—the colored bars show the percentage of a country's total labor force that works in agriculture. The overlaid black boxes show the percentage of a country's gross domestic product that comes from agriculture. In most cases—except Argentina—the number of agricultural workers far exceeds the amount of income produced by the farming industry.

GRAPH 2 depicts the percentage of paved roads, while GRAPH 3 illustrates the inflation rate. The inflation figures for Colombia, Guyana, and Brazil are estimated. GRAPH 4 depicts two aspects of energy usage. The left half of a country's bar is the percentage of energy from fossil fuel (oil or coal); the right half shows the percentage of energy from hydropower. In GRAPH 5, which depicts distribution of wealth, each country's bar represents 100 percent of its total income. The top section is the portion of income received by the richest 10 percent of the population. The bottom section is the portion received by the poorest 20 percent. GRAPH 6 represents the percentage of homes that have electricity.

money to firms that are too large to be financed by private investors. The IFI encourages the production of goods that are usually imported and that use a lot of national raw materials. Metalworking and automobile assembly plants, and firms that produce paper, vegetable oils, and petroleum derivatives have attracted IFI funds.

Home appliances still form the backbone of Colombia's manufacturing economy. Nevertheless, small factories turn out beer, clothing, cigarettes, soap, shoes, cement, pharmaceuticals, chemical products, fertilizers, and rubber and leather articles to an increasing market.

Mineral and Fuel Resources

Colombia is extremely rich in minerals, including gold, salt, coal, nickel, silver, copper, lead, mercury, manganese, and platinum. Moreover, the nation is the world's leading producer of emeralds—a valuable gemstone. The chief known emerald deposits are at Muzo and Chivor. Gold is found chiefly in Antioquia, and salt comes from both the Zipaquirá mines— which are several hundred feet deep and which occupy several hundred square miles —and from sea-salt pans on the Caribbean coast.

A valuable commerical deposit of coal that is clean (low in sulfur, so it burns without creating pollution), that is near the surface, and that can be mined using open-pit or strip-mining techniques is located on La Guajira Peninusula. The Colombian government, Exxon Corporation, and Morrison-Knudsen Construction Company together have spent $3.5 million to

The salt mines at Zipaquirá are so vast that a cathedral was built underground in a hollowed-out gallery. The 75-foot-high ceiling arches over an 18-ton block of salt that is used as the main altar.

La Esmeralda dam in Chivor Canyon near Guateque, central Colombia, produces over one million kilowatts of electric power annually. At 777 feet high, the dam is the third highest rock dam in Latin America.

develop an open-pit mine in this area. Colombia may have as much as 60 percent of South America's coal reserves.

Oil production began in the early twentieth century in the Magdalena River Valley, which still supplies most of the nation's crude oil. A refinery at Barrancabermeja accounts for much of the cargo traffic in Magdalena. Other oil deposits have been found in the basin of the Catatumbo River, in the central Caribbean and Pacific areas, in the eastern llanos, and in the Amazon region. Colombia exported more than 250,000 barrels of oil a day in the late 1980s. To the nation's economy, oil is becoming as valuable as coffee.

Energy

Colombia is trying to keep pace with its growing energy demands by harnessing the power of its many waterways. Experts claim that, because of the nation's heavy rainfall and many rivers, Colombia has one of the highest hydroelectric potentials in the world. The drier, northern regions along the coast, however, increasingly use thermal energy and natural gas.

Cali is the headquarters of the Cauca Valley Authority, which was organized with the assistance of the United States. The corporation's major concerns are flood control, development of electrical power, improved farm techniques, and irrigation. As evidence of its success, the corpora-

A mountainous road from Bogotá to the outlying village of Choachí demonstrates the difficulty in constructing thoroughfares that will crisscross Colombia.

Photo by Amandus Schneider

tion tripled Cali's electrical power within eight years.

Transportation

Bolivia is the only other country on the South American continent with transportation problems as difficult as those of Colombia. High mountains make the construction of roads and railways in Colombia difficult and expensive to develop. In some areas mules or aerial cable cars are the only means used for transporting goods and people across difficult terrain.

Inland waterways are very important. Before the railway from Santa Marta to Bogotá was built, the Magdalena River was the major route between the Caribbean and the interior. Drought, however, prevents travel on the Magdalena during the dry season. A railway connects La Dorada on the Magdalena with Santa Marta on the Caribbean coast. The country's 2,100-mile rail system, which was nation-

Courtesy of World Bank

Flooding is a common problem in rural Colombia, but this bus crosses a stream to keep on schedule.

alized in 1954 and is almost all government owned, continues to expand. The Pacific Railway connects Bogotá with the port of Buenaventura. An Atlantic rail line from Bogotá to Santa Marta was opened in 1961.

Colombia's currently inadequate highway system is being improved to connect all major cities with the Caribbean and Pacific coasts. The country's three most important road systems are the western, central, and eastern highways, which run north to south between the mountain ranges. The 2,300-mile Simon Bolívar Highway runs from Caracas, Venezuela, to Santiago de Guayaquil, Ecuador. The Pacific port of Buenaventura is linked to Cali by the Carretera al Mar. A section of the Pan-American Highway extends between Cali, Bogotá, and Venezuela.

In order to overcome its mountainous terrain, Colombia became a pioneer in civil aviation. Between 1919 and 1920 German interests began a domestic airline service, which later became Avianca, Colombia's major international airline.

The Future

Colombia has varied and extensive resources that—if developed—could help to make it self-sufficient. The nation has a relatively small foreign debt and widespread outside investment. Thus, Colombia has fewer financial limitations than many of its South American neighbors. But export prices for coffee—the country's most important legal export—are no longer stable. Coffee prices dropped with the suspension in 1989 of an international coffee agreement. This loss has been offset somewhat by the nation's ability to export more oil. In addition, government steps to combat the problem of drug trafficking, which causes corruption and violence, is costly. Colombia's struggle to regain and preserve its democracy will be a major feature in the coming decade.

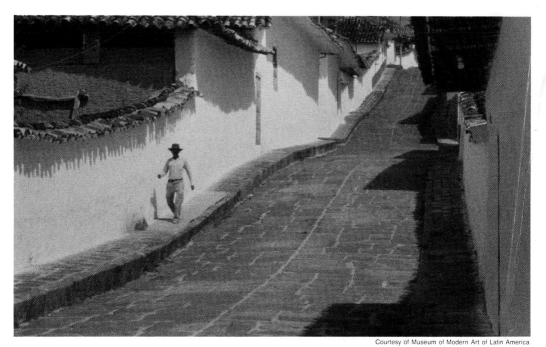

The streets of Barichara, a village of the Colombian Andes, are treeless, narrow thoroughfares. This street follows the natural contours of the sloping terrain.

Index